LIFE CYCLE OF A...
Honey Bee

Words in **bold** can be found in the glossary on page 24.

©2016
Book Life
King's Lynn
Norfolk PE30 4LS

ISBN: 978-1-910512-47-0

Written by:
Grace Jones
Edited by:
Amy Allatson
Designed by:
Matt Rumbelow

A catalogue record for this book
is available from the British Library.

LIFE CYCLE OF A...
Honey Bee

What is a Life Cycle?

All animals, **insects** and humans go through different stages of their life as they grow and change. This is called a **life cycle**.

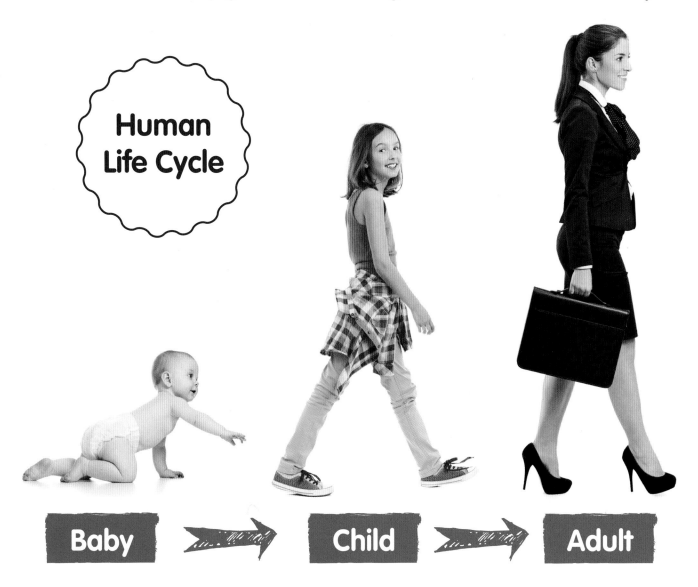

Human Life Cycle

Baby → Child → Adult

What is a Bee?

A bee is an insect. It has four wings that it uses to fly, five eyes and six legs.

Eyes

Wings

Legs

Eggs

The **queen bee** lays her eggs on a ball of **pollen** inside her home. A bee's home is called a hive.

A queen honey bee laying eggs.

Eggs

The queen bee covers the eggs with wax to keep them safe. She lays up to two thousand eggs a day.

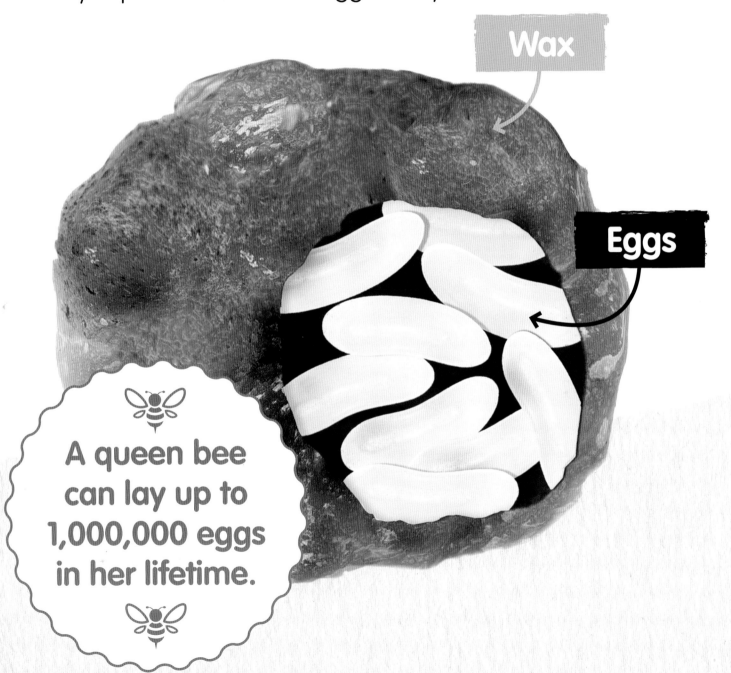

Wax

Eggs

A queen bee can lay up to 1,000,000 eggs in her lifetime.

Grubs

The Queen bee sits on her eggs in the hive to keep them warm. She drinks a sweet, sugary liquid called nectar for food.

There is only ever one queen bee in each hive.

After around four days, the bee eggs **hatch** and small,
white grubs called **larvae** wriggle out of their eggshells.

Larvae

Growing Grubs

The grubs eat the pollen underneath them for their food. The queen bee leaves the hive and flies away to find more food for the hungry grubs to eat.

A bee looking for food

There are up to 60,000 larvae in each hive.

The grubs grow so quickly that their skin gets too tight and small for their bodies. They **shed** their old skin and grow new, bigger skin underneath.

Changing Grubs

Once the grub has grown big enough, it spins a coat of silk around itself. This is called a cocoon.

Cocoon

Inside the cocoon, the grub is changing into a bee. It sheds its skin one more time before it is ready to come out.

Inside the hive, the grub is changing into a bee.

Bees

When the bee is fully grown, it chews its way out of its cocoon.
It is now ready to start its adult life.

There are three types of bee living in the hive; the queen bee, worker bees and drone bees.

Drone Bee

Worker Bee

Brilliant Bees

Honey bees make the sweet honey that we eat and buy in shops. Honey is made from the nectar the worker bees collect from flowers.

Honey

There are over 25,000 different types of bees in the world.

Bees speak to each other by doing a special sort of dance in the air. This is called the waggle dance.

Looking for Food

Worker bees collect nectar and pollen for their food and bring it back to the hive for the other bees to eat. Nectar and pollen is found in the flowers of a plant.

Nectar from flowers.

Worker bees carry pollen in special baskets on their legs.

Worker Bee

Honey bees look for brightly coloured flowers to find nectar and pollen. They drink it using their long tongues, which they use just like a straw!

The World's Largest Bee Hive:
Found In Texas, USA
Size: Over 6m Long

6m

Fun Fact: The biggest bee hive ever found had over 500,000 bees in it.

The World's Largest Bee:

Female Leafcutter Bee

Size: 3.8cm

Fun Fact: The Leafcutter Bee is found in Indonesia and they build their hives in termite nests.

Life Cycle of a Honey Bee

1 A queen bee lays eggs in a hive.

2 A grub hatches from an egg.

LIFE CYCLES

4 The grub has changed into an adult bee.

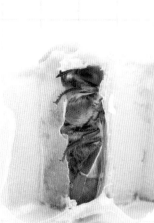

3 The grub wraps itself in a silk cocoon inside its home.

Get Exploring!

See if you can spot any bees in your garden or local park.

The best time to look for bees is in the summer when it is warm and sunny. Are they doing the waggle dance? Be very careful not to get near to the bees you see, they might sting you.

Glossary

Hatch: When a young animal or insect comes out of its egg.

Insect: Minibeasts that have six legs and four wings.

Pollen: A yellow powder that is found in a flower.

Queen Bee: A female bee who is in charge of the hive and the only bee who can lay eggs.

Shed: When an insect's old skin falls off.

Index